Growing Readers

Purchased with Smart Start Funds

# first book about animals

# of the forests

For a free color catalog describing Gareth Stevens' list of high-quality books and multimedia programs, call 1-800-542-2595 (USA) or 1-800-461-9120 (Canada). Gareth Stevens Publishing's Fax: (414) 225-0377.

Library of Congress Cataloging-in-Publication Data available upon request from publisher.  Fax: (414) 225-0377 for the attention of the Publishing Records Department.

ISBN 0-8368-2650-7

This North American edition first published in 2000 by
**Gareth Stevens Publishing**
1555 North RiverCenter Drive, Suite 201
Milwaukee, WI  53212  USA

Created and produced as *visit the animals in the forests* by QA International,
329 rue de la Commune Ouest, 3e étage,
Montréal, Québec, Canada  H2Y 2E1.
Tel.: (514) 499-3000 Fax: (514) 499-3010
www.qa-international.com

Printed in the United States of America

1 2 3 4 5 6 7 8 9 04 03 02 01 00

Gareth Stevens Publishing
**MILWAUKEE**

The chimpanzees...

2

are having fun with their friends.

3

# The snail travels...

# with its house on its back.

# The panda loves...

to eat bamboo.

# The wolf is howling...

# at the moon.

# The skunk is raising...

its furry tail.

The peacock is showing off...

its magnificent feathers.

# The koala is sitting...

on a branch to eat.

# Glossary

**bamboo** — a type of tall grass with hard, hollow stems.

**friends** — people you like and enjoy spending time with.

**howling** — making a loud, wailing noise.

**koala** — a small, furry animal from Australia that lives in eucalyptus trees.

**magnificent** — wonderful; awesome.

**moon** — the celestial body that circles Earth.

**travel** — to go from one place to another; to make a journey.

# Index